Microsoft Loop

The Microsoft 365 Companion Series

Dr. Patrick Jones

OLYMPUS ACADEMY
PRESS

TABLE OF CONTENTS

WORK TOGETHER, STAY CONNECTED

In today's fast-paced world, teamwork and collaboration are the keys to success. But as teams grow and tasks become more complex, keeping everyone on the same page can feel like chasing shadows. Notes get buried, files are scattered, and important updates get lost in the noise. What if there was a tool that brought everything—and everyone—together, seamlessly? Enter Microsoft Loop, a dynamic app that redefines collaboration for the modern workplace.

Microsoft Loop isn't just another tool; it's a game-changer for how people work together. Designed to integrate effortlessly with the Microsoft 365 ecosystem, Loop enables real-time collaboration, flexible content sharing, and seamless communication—no matter where your team is or what tools they use. Whether you're brainstorming ideas, managing projects, or co-authoring documents, Loop ensures that the right information is always in the right place at the right time.

Unlike traditional collaboration tools that lock your content into static documents, Microsoft Loop breaks free. At its heart, Loop consists of:

- **Loop Components:** Small, adaptable pieces of content—like checklists, tables, or notes—that live in chats, emails, and documents, staying in sync no matter where they appear.

- **Loop Workspaces:** A shared space for your team to organize, manage, and contribute to projects, ensuring everyone stays aligned.

- **Loop Pages:** Flexible canvases that bring Loop Components and other content together, providing a collaborative hub for your ideas and tasks.

This dynamic, modular approach allows Loop to evolve alongside your team's needs. It's not just a place to work—it's where your work moves forward, piece by piece, idea by idea.

The modern workplace is a web of tools, conversations, and projects happening all at once. Without a central, flexible way to connect content and people, important information can slip through the cracks. Microsoft Loop solves that problem by creating a unified, living workspace where collaboration is effortless and adaptable.

Imagine this:

- A task list shared in a Teams chat updates in real-time, whether someone views it in Loop, Teams, or Outlook.

- A project status table can live simultaneously in a Loop Page, your team's meeting notes, and an email, staying perfectly in sync everywhere it's accessed.

- Your team's brainstorming ideas can start as a Loop Page and grow into structured tasks with actionable steps—without ever leaving the platform.

In short, Loop doesn't ask your team to change how they work; it adapts to how you already collaborate, seamlessly integrating with tools like Microsoft Teams, Outlook, and OneDrive.

This book is your friendly guide to understanding, adopting, and mastering Microsoft Loop. With clear explanations, practical examples, and relatable scenarios, you'll learn how to:

- Understand the fundamentals of Microsoft Loop and its role in modern collaboration.

- Use Loop Components to create adaptable content that syncs in real-time across tools.

- Organize and manage workspaces to keep your projects on track and your team aligned.

- Integrate Loop seamlessly with Microsoft Teams, Outlook, and other Microsoft 365 tools.

- Explore Copilot in Loop for AI-powered suggestions and smarter collaboration workflows.

- Avoid common pitfalls and maximize your team's productivity with best practices and time-saving tips.

Throughout the book, you'll follow Sarah's journey as she discovers Microsoft Loop, transforms her team's workflows, and overcomes the challenges of scattered communication and misaligned tasks. Sarah's story will serve as an inspiration—and a practical example—of how you can use Loop to simplify teamwork and stay connected.

In the coming chapters, we'll explore exactly what Microsoft Loop is, why it's such a valuable tool, and how you can start using it to revolutionize the way you and your team work. Whether you're collaborating with a small team on a creative project or managing a large, multi-department initiative, Microsoft Loop gives you the flexibility and structure you need to succeed.

Let's dive in and start your journey toward smarter, more connected teamwork. With Microsoft Loop, your collaboration has no limits!

WHAT IS MICROSOFT LOOP?

In the ever-evolving landscape of workplace tools, Microsoft Loop stands out as a fresh and powerful way to connect people, content, and ideas in a unified, collaborative space. Designed with flexibility and real-time synchronization at its core, Loop transforms the way teams share, update, and manage information—no matter where they're working or which Microsoft 365 app they're using.

At its heart, Microsoft Loop is a dynamic, modular tool built to solve one of today's biggest workplace challenges: how to keep everyone aligned, engaged, and productive while working across multiple apps and platforms. It's not just about documents or files; it's about creating a connected ecosystem where content isn't static—it's living, breathing, and evolving alongside your team.

Microsoft Loop is made up of three main building blocks:

1. **Loop Components**
   Loop Components are the flexible, interactive pieces of content that form the backbone of Loop. These components can be as simple as a checklist, a table, or meeting notes, or as complex as task lists and progress trackers.

What makes them unique? They stay in sync wherever you use them. If a Loop Component is shared in an Outlook email, a Microsoft Teams chat, or a Loop Page, any updates you make are instantly reflected everywhere it lives.

- o **Examples of Loop Components:**
  - **Checklists:** Track to-dos across teams with a list that updates in real time.
  - **Tables:** Organize data collaboratively, such as tracking project statuses.
  - **Notes:** Take shared meeting notes that everyone can edit live.

- **Progress Trackers:** Visualize the status of tasks or milestones dynamically.

Example: Sarah created a task list component in a Teams chat for her team's project. When a teammate updated the list in Outlook, the changes appeared instantly in Teams and on Sarah's Loop Page.

2. **Loop Pages**

   A Loop Page is where your components come together. Think of it as a flexible workspace—similar to a digital whiteboard or notebook—where your team can create, organize, and collaborate.

On a Loop Page, you can bring in Loop Components, files, links, and other content, all in one place. It's like a hub for your ideas and tasks, allowing everyone to work together on a single page without losing focus.

   o Use Loop Pages for:

       - Brainstorming ideas with your team.

       - Organizing project tasks, timelines, and resources.

       - Creating a living document that updates as your project progresses.

Example: Sarah set up a Loop Page for her team's product launch, including a timeline table, brainstorming notes, and a checklist for deliverables. Everyone contributed updates in real time, creating a unified space for the project.

3. **Loop Workspaces**

   A Loop Workspace is the big picture—a shared space where you and your team can group Loop Pages and organize everything related to a project. Workspaces keep everyone aligned by consolidating your project's content and progress into a single, accessible location.

- o Use Workspaces to:
    - Bring multiple Loop Pages together under one project or team goal.
    - Organize all your components, documents, and links into one space.
    - Keep team members up to date with project activity and contributions.

Example: Sarah's team created a Loop Workspace called "Q4 Marketing Plan," which included individual Pages for campaign brainstorming, task assignments, and budget tracking. It was their single source of truth for the entire project.

Microsoft Loop isn't a standalone tool—it's deeply integrated into the Microsoft 365 ecosystem, allowing you to work seamlessly across apps like Teams, Outlook, Word, and OneDrive. Loop brings content to life wherever you need it:

- In **Teams chats**, where a checklist component helps teams track their to-dos.
- In **Outlook emails**, where a table component ensures everyone has the most updated data.
- In **SharePoint**, where Loop components link directly to larger project spaces.
- In **OneDrive**, where Loop Pages are securely stored and accessible anytime.

This integration means that you don't need to switch between apps to update a task, note, or table—Loop keeps everything connected and updated, no matter where you're working.

Traditional documents are static. You create a file, share it, and hope your team uses the "right version." Microsoft Loop changes this. Loop Components are living content—updated in real time and always current, no matter where they're embedded.

This dynamic nature ensures:

- **No version chaos:** Say goodbye to "final_final_v2" filenames. Everyone sees the latest updates, instantly.

- **Faster collaboration:** Teams can update checklists, notes, and data on the fly without waiting for updates or digging through emails.

- **Improved productivity:** Loop eliminates the need to recreate or re-share content across tools.

Example: Sarah's team used a Loop table to track tasks during a project. Whether a team member updated the table in Teams or on a Loop Page, the changes were immediate. It became their single, reliable source of truth.

The beauty of Microsoft Loop lies in its accessibility. Whether you're part of a small team, a large organization, or even working solo, Loop adapts to your needs.

- **Small Teams:** Loop is perfect for brainstorming sessions, task tracking, and shared planning.

- **Large Organizations:** Workspaces and Pages scale to organize complex projects across departments.

- **Individuals:** Use Loop Pages to manage personal projects, organize notes, or track goals.

With its real-time sync and modular design, Loop removes barriers to effective teamwork.

In a digital world full of scattered tools and disconnected information, Microsoft Loop bridges the gap between content, people, and platforms. It's the answer to a growing need for flexible, connected, and dynamic collaboration tools that keep up with the way we work today.

With Loop, teams can:

- Work together effortlessly.
- Keep content up to date in real time.
- Stay aligned, no matter where or how they work.

Now that you understand what Microsoft Loop is and how it works, you're ready to explore why it's such a valuable tool for teams and individuals alike.

WHY USE MICROSOFT LOOP?

Collaboration has never been more critical—or more challenging—than it is today. With teams working across different locations, time zones, and platforms, keeping everyone aligned and productive can feel like an uphill battle. Notes get scattered, updates are missed, and static documents fail to keep pace with the speed of work. That's where Microsoft Loop steps in.

Microsoft Loop isn't just another collaboration tool; it's a dynamic, living workspace that evolves with your projects and connects seamlessly with the Microsoft 365 ecosystem. It's designed to help teams work smarter, communicate effortlessly, and stay organized, no matter where they are or how they collaborate.

This chapter explores why Microsoft Loop is a game-changer for individuals and teams, highlighting its unique benefits and real-world applications.

1. Living, Dynamic Content

One of the standout features of Microsoft Loop is its ability to create "living content"—information that stays in sync no matter where it's shared. Whether you're editing a checklist in Teams, an email in Outlook, or a Loop Page, any changes you make are reflected instantly everywhere the component lives.

Why It Matters:

- **Goodbye version chaos:** No more chasing down the latest version of a file or document. Everyone always has the most up-to-date information.

- **Reduced duplication:** A single Loop Component can appear in multiple places (e.g., Teams chats, Outlook emails) without being recreated or copied.

- **Real-time updates:** Changes are visible immediately, keeping everyone on the same page, literally and figuratively.

Example: Sarah's team managed a shared task list using a Loop Component embedded in Teams and Outlook. As team members updated tasks in either location, the changes synced instantly. No more outdated checklists or missed updates.

2. Seamless Integration Across Microsoft 365

Microsoft Loop doesn't exist in isolation. It integrates seamlessly with Microsoft Teams, Outlook, OneDrive, and other Microsoft 365 tools, becoming the connective tissue between your apps.

Why It Matters:

- **Work where you are:** You don't need to jump between apps to update content—Loop Components adapt to where you're working.

- **Cross-platform collaboration:** Whether you're on Teams, editing an email in Outlook, or organizing content in a Loop Workspace, Loop follows you wherever you go.

- **Unified experience:** Loop eliminates silos, connecting your tools and workflows into one streamlined system.

Example: During a team meeting in Microsoft Teams, Sarah added a Loop table to track project deadlines. Later, she embedded the same table into a follow-up email in Outlook. Team members who missed the meeting could still access and update the table directly from the email.

3. Flexible and Adaptable Workspaces

Traditional tools often force teams into rigid workflows or static documents. Microsoft Loop takes a different approach, offering flexible Pages and Workspaces where teams can brainstorm, plan, and manage projects in a way that works for them.

Why It Matters:

- **Freedom to organize:** Build Loop Pages with checklists, notes, tables, and files that adapt to your needs.

- **Customizable Workspaces:** Group related Pages together in a Loop Workspace to keep projects organized and accessible.

- **Collaboration for all styles:** Whether you're a visual planner, a note-taker, or a list-maker, Loop provides the tools to work your way.

Example: Sarah created a Loop Workspace for her team's product launch. Each Loop Page served a specific purpose—brainstorming ideas, tracking deadlines, and managing budgets. The team could work together in one space without feeling overwhelmed.

4. Streamlined Collaboration for Remote and Hybrid Teams

In today's hybrid work environment, staying connected can be a challenge. Microsoft Loop bridges the gap, enabling teams to collaborate effectively whether they're in the same room or working across the globe.

Why It Matters:

- **Real-time teamwork:** Edit, comment, and brainstorm with your team in real time.

- **Reduced friction:** Updates appear instantly, ensuring everyone sees changes as they happen.

- **Improved alignment:** Keep team members aligned with shared Workspaces and Pages that centralize project information.

Example: Sarah's remote team collaborated on a marketing campaign in a shared Loop Workspace. Team members in different time zones contributed ideas to the same Loop Page, allowing everyone to see updates and stay aligned without multiple follow-up emails.

5. Saves Time and Reduces Duplication

Loop streamlines your workflows by eliminating repetitive tasks and reducing the need to recreate or reformat content.

Why It Matters:

- **Reusable components:** Loop Components can be embedded anywhere, saving time and effort.

- **Centralized updates:** Edit a component once, and changes appear everywhere it's used.

- **Faster collaboration:** Real-time updates mean less back-and-forth communication and fewer delays.

Example: Sarah embedded a Loop Component of meeting notes in multiple places—a Teams chat, a Loop Page, and an email. As the notes were updated, the changes synced automatically, saving time and reducing manual work.

6. Enhances Project Management and Organization

With Loop's modular structure, teams can manage projects and tasks with clarity and precision. From brainstorming ideas to tracking progress, Loop simplifies project workflows.

Why It Matters:

- **Track tasks and milestones:** Use Loop Components like checklists, tables, and progress trackers to monitor project progress.

- **Organize content visually:** Combine multiple components into a single Loop Page to keep everything in one place.

- **Stay on schedule:** Dynamic updates ensure everyone knows what's next and who's responsible.

Example: Sarah's team managed a content calendar in a Loop table. As deadlines approached, the table updated dynamically, helping team members stay on top of their tasks.

7. Built for the Future of Collaboration

Microsoft Loop is designed for the way people work today and in the future. Its integration with AI-powered tools like Copilot adds another layer of efficiency and innovation.

- **Smarter collaboration:** Copilot in Loop can suggest content, summarize updates, and automate repetitive tasks.
- **Adapts to change:** Loop's flexibility allows it to grow with your team's needs, adapting to new challenges and workflows.

Example: Sarah used Copilot in Loop to summarize brainstorming notes into actionable tasks, saving her team time and effort during their planning phase.

Microsoft Loop is more than just another productivity tool—it's a better way to work, collaborate, and organize your ideas. By integrating dynamic content, seamless updates, and flexible workspaces, Loop transforms how individuals and teams approach their work.

- For teams, Loop reduces friction, improves communication, and keeps everyone aligned.
- For leaders, it offers clarity and transparency to manage projects effectively.
- For individuals, it simplifies workflows and makes collaboration intuitive and stress-free.

Now that you understand why Microsoft Loop is such a valuable tool, it's time to learn how to get started.

YOUR FIRST STEPS

So you're ready to dive into Microsoft Loop, but where do you begin? Whether you're an individual user exploring a better way to organize your ideas or part of a team looking to revolutionize collaboration, Microsoft Loop provides an intuitive, flexible starting point. This chapter will guide you step-by-step through the basics of setting up and using Loop so you can start creating dynamic, synchronized content today.

By the end of this chapter, you'll know how to:

- Access Microsoft Loop and set up your environment.

- Create your first Loop Components, Pages, and Workspaces.

- Share content seamlessly across Microsoft 365 apps.

Let's get started!

1. Accessing Microsoft Loop

To begin, you need access to Microsoft Loop. Because Loop is part of the Microsoft 365 ecosystem, you can use it through a supported Microsoft 365 account.

- **From the Web:** Go to loop.microsoft.com and sign in using your Microsoft 365 credentials.

- **In Microsoft Teams:** Open a Teams chat, meeting, or channel and embed Loop Components directly.

- **In Outlook and Word:** Loop Components integrate naturally into emails and documents as dynamic content.

If your organization doesn't have Loop enabled, contact your IT administrator to ensure Loop is available for your account.

2. Setting Up Your First Workspace

Loop Workspaces act as your central hub, where all related content and collaboration happen.

Steps to Create a Workspace:

1. Go to the Loop homepage.

2. Click on "Create a Workspace" to start a new project.

3. Name your workspace. Choose something clear and descriptive, like "Marketing Campaign Q4" or "Weekly Team Updates."

4. (Optional) Add a cover image or color theme to personalize your workspace.

5. Invite team members by adding their email addresses.

Tips:

- Start small: Create workspaces for individual projects, teams, or specific goals.

- Use clear, actionable names to keep your workspaces organized.

Example: Sarah created a workspace called *"Client Onboarding Process"* for her team, bringing together meeting notes, task lists, and status trackers into a unified location.

3. Creating Your First Loop Page

Once your workspace is ready, you can create Loop Pages. Think of these pages as digital canvases where you'll organize your content, from simple notes to structured tasks.

Steps to Create a Page:

1. Open your workspace and click "New Page" to create a blank canvas.

2. Name your page. For example: *"Brainstorming Notes," "Project Timeline,"* or *"Meeting Agenda."*

3. Add content to the page:

- o Click anywhere on the page to insert Loop Components, text, files, or links.

- o Use the + (Add Component) menu to add interactive elements like checklists, tables, or progress trackers.

Example: Sarah created a Loop Page called *"Team Check-In"* for her weekly meetings. It included a note-taking component, a checklist for action items, and a progress tracker for ongoing tasks.

4. Introducing Loop Components

Loop Components are the true magic of Microsoft Loop. They're flexible, interactive pieces of content—like checklists, tables, or notes—that can be embedded in multiple places and updated in real time.

How to Create a Loop Component:

1. On your Loop Page, click the + icon or type "/" to open the components menu.

2. Select the type of component you want to add:

   - o **Checklist**: Perfect for to-dos and task tracking.

   - o **Table**: Great for organizing data and sharing project statuses.

   - o **Notes**: A simple way to take live, shared notes.

   - o **Progress Tracker**: Ideal for monitoring goals and milestones.

3. Start editing the component. As you make updates, the changes will reflect immediately wherever the component is shared.

Sharing Loop Components in Other Apps:

- Copy a Loop Component and paste it into a Teams chat, an Outlook email, or even Word.

- Wherever it lives, the component will stay in sync across platforms.

Example: Sarah created a task list in a Loop Page for her product launch. She shared the same component in a Teams channel and an Outlook email. When a teammate checked off a task in Teams, the update was visible immediately in Outlook and on the Loop Page.

5. Collaborating with Your Team

Loop shines brightest when teams work together. Collaboration happens in real time, with updates appearing instantly for everyone.

Key Collaboration Features:

- **Live Editing:** Multiple people can edit the same Loop Page or Component simultaneously. Changes appear immediately, so there's no confusion about who updated what.

- **Comments and Feedback:** Add comments to any component or section to provide feedback and track discussions.

- **Notifications:** Team members get notified of changes or updates made to shared Loop Components.

Example: During a brainstorming session, Sarah's team used a shared Loop Page to jot down ideas in real time. Teammates added notes and suggestions, while Sarah left comments to clarify action points.

6. Saving and Organizing Content

Organization is key to making the most of Loop. As your workspaces and pages grow, keeping everything tidy ensures you and your team can stay focused.

Tips for Organization:

- Use clear and consistent naming for Pages and Components.

- Group related Loop Pages into Workspaces based on projects or goals.
- Archive old Pages or Workspaces that are no longer needed to keep your environment clean.

Example: Sarah created folders within her workspace to separate content: one for meeting notes, another for brainstorming sessions, and one for project updates.

7. Integrating Microsoft Loop Across Apps

One of Loop's greatest strengths is its ability to work seamlessly across Microsoft 365 apps:

- **In Teams:** Paste Loop Components into chats, meetings, or channels for instant collaboration.
- **In Outlook:** Embed Loop Components in emails to keep everyone updated with live content.
- **In Word and OneNote:** Use Loop Components as dynamic, living content that stays up to date wherever it's shared.

Congratulations! You now have the foundation you need to start using Microsoft Loop effectively. From creating your first workspace to embedding components across apps, you're ready to experience the power of living, connected content.

WORK SMARTER, COLLABORATE BETTER

Microsoft Loop is an incredibly versatile and dynamic tool, but like any collaboration platform, it works best when used with intention and structure. To get the most out of Loop, it's important to follow best practices that streamline workflows, improve team communication, and maximize productivity.

In this chapter, we'll cover practical tips, strategies, and insights to help you work smarter with Loop—whether you're organizing projects, creating components, or collaborating with your team.

1. Start with a Clear Purpose for Each Workspace

Workspaces are the foundation of Microsoft Loop, acting as centralized hubs for projects and ideas. However, without a clear purpose, workspaces can quickly become cluttered or disorganized.

Best Practices:

- **Define the Goal:** Before creating a workspace, determine its purpose. Is it for a project, a team, or a brainstorming session?

- **Use Descriptive Names:** Give your workspace a clear, recognizable name. For example: *"Q1 Marketing Plan"* or *"Weekly Team Updates."*

- **Limit Workspaces:** Avoid creating too many workspaces for minor tasks. Group related pages under one workspace to keep things manageable.

Example: Sarah's team created a single workspace called *"Client Onboarding Process,"* which contained pages for meeting notes, task lists, and project timelines. This prevented her team from scattering documents across multiple workspaces.

2. Keep Loop Pages Focused and Organized

A Loop Page is your blank canvas, but without structure, it can become overwhelming.

Best Practices:

- **One Purpose, One Page:** Each Loop Page should have a clear purpose. For example, use one page for meeting notes, another for brainstorming, and another for project status updates.

- **Use Headings and Sections:** Break content into sections with headings to improve readability and navigation.

- **Embed the Right Components:** Only include relevant components—like task lists, tables, or notes—to avoid clutter.

- **Add Links for Context:** Use hyperlinks to connect related pages, files, or external resources.

Example: During her project kickoff, Sarah created a "Meeting Notes" page that included a live checklist, notes section, and relevant links to client files. The clean layout kept her team focused and organized.

3. Master Loop Components for Dynamic Collaboration

Loop Components are where the magic happens. Since they sync in real time, they can be reused across apps while staying up to date.

Best Practices:

- **Choose the Right Component:** Pick the component that fits your needs—checklists for to-dos, tables for structured data, and notes for freeform ideas.

- **Reuse Components Effectively:** Share the same component in multiple places (Teams, Outlook, Loop Pages) to reduce duplication and ensure updates are synced everywhere.

- **Keep Components Concise:** Avoid overcrowding components with too much content; focus on actionable or essential information.

- **Track Updates:** Use comments or highlight changes to draw attention to updates in shared components.

Example: Sarah embedded a task list component in her project's Loop Page and also shared it in a Teams chat. As teammates updated the list in Teams, it reflected in real time on the Loop Page, keeping everyone aligned.

4. Collaborate in Real Time, But Respect Boundaries

Real-time collaboration is one of Microsoft Loop's superpowers, but too many simultaneous edits can sometimes lead to confusion.

Best Practices:

- **Communicate Clearly:** Let teammates know what you're editing to avoid overwriting each other's work.

- **Use Comments Wisely:** Instead of making direct edits, leave comments to provide feedback or suggestions.

- **Set Page Guidelines:** For complex pages, agree on roles (e.g., one person edits notes, another manages tasks).

Example: During a brainstorming session, Sarah's team left comments on ideas instead of editing the content directly, keeping the original notes intact while adding feedback.

5. Integrate Loop Seamlessly Across Microsoft 365

Loop works best when it's integrated with your existing Microsoft tools like Teams, Outlook, and Word.

Best Practices:

- **Embed Components in Teams:** Use Loop Components in Teams chats and meetings to streamline real-time collaboration.

- **Utilize Outlook:** Include Loop Components in emails for dynamic content that doesn't require multiple follow-ups.

- **Store Files in OneDrive or SharePoint:** Keep files linked to your Loop Pages organized and accessible through cloud storage.

- **Leverage Word and Whiteboard:** Incorporate Loop Components into Word for reports or into Whiteboard for visual collaboration.

Example: Sarah shared a Loop table component in a Teams meeting to track project milestones. Afterward, she added the same table to an Outlook email summary, ensuring everyone could access and update it in either location.

6. Use Copilot to Streamline Content Creation

Copilot, the AI-powered assistant in Microsoft Loop, can transform how you create and organize your content.

Best Practices:

- **Ask for Suggestions:** Use Copilot to brainstorm ideas, summarize long notes, or create structured content like checklists or timelines.

- **Simplify Updates:** Let Copilot suggest edits or highlight changes for clarity.

- **Summarize Meeting Notes:** After a brainstorming session, ask Copilot to pull key takeaways and turn them into actionable tasks.

Example: After a lengthy brainstorming session, Sarah asked Copilot to summarize the team's discussion and generate a to-do list. It saved her hours of manual work and kept the team focused.

7. Avoid Overloading Pages and Workspaces

While Loop is flexible, overloading it with too much information can make pages and workspaces harder to navigate.

Best Practices:

- **Keep Pages Simple:** Avoid packing too many components or sections into one page.

- **Archive Unused Content:** If a page or component is no longer needed, archive it or move it to a "Completed" folder.

- **Review Regularly:** Periodically clean up workspaces to remove outdated or irrelevant content.

Example: Sarah archived old Loop Pages from a completed project to keep her team's workspace focused on current initiatives.

8. Create a Workflow That Works for Your Team

No two teams work the same way, and Microsoft Loop is designed to adapt to your unique needs.

Best Practices:

- **Agree on Standards:** Define how your team will use Loop (e.g., naming conventions, component placement, etc.).

- **Assign Ownership:** Ensure someone is responsible for maintaining and updating Loop Pages or components.

- **Iterate as You Go:** Start simple and refine your workflows as your team becomes more familiar with Loop.

Example: Sarah's team agreed to name all task-related pages *"[Project Name] Tasks"* for consistency, making it easier to navigate workspaces.

By following these best practices, you'll make Microsoft Loop a powerful asset in your productivity toolkit. With clear organization, smart use of components, and seamless collaboration, you'll reduce confusion, boost efficiency, and keep your projects on track.

UNLOCK HIDDEN POTENTIAL

Microsoft Loop is more than just another productivity tool—it's a dynamic workspace designed to evolve with the way you work. While you may already be familiar with the basics, there are plenty of tips, tricks, and clever techniques that can help you unlock the true power of Loop. Whether you're working solo, leading a team, or managing a complex project, these tips will help you save time, stay organized, and boost collaboration.

1. Use Shortcuts to Work Faster

Did you know Microsoft Loop has keyboard shortcuts and quick commands to speed up your work? Instead of clicking through menus, you can type shortcuts or commands to add components, format text, and stay focused on what matters.

- **Type "/" to Insert Components:**
  Pressing the "/" key brings up a list of available Loop Components—like checklists, tables, and notes—allowing you to quickly insert and customize what you need.

    o Example: Type /checklist to instantly add a task list component.

Tip: Keep a cheat sheet of your favorite shortcuts nearby until they become second nature.

2. Use Loop Components as Real-Time Dashboards

Transform Loop Components into living dashboards to track progress, monitor tasks, and share updates across tools.

- **Task Lists:** Use a checklist component for team to-dos. Assign owners and deadlines, and watch progress in real time as items are checked off.

- **Status Tables:** Use a table component to track project milestones, team assignments, or resource allocation. Add columns for status updates (e.g., "In Progress," "Complete").

- **Progress Trackers:** Include a progress tracker component to visualize your team's overall progress.

Example: Sarah created a real-time dashboard for her product launch that included a task list, a project timeline, and a notes section. She shared it in Teams and Outlook to ensure her team always had access to the latest updates.

3. Embed Loop Components Everywhere

Loop Components are designed to sync across Microsoft 365 apps, so don't limit them to your Loop workspace—embed them where your team already works.

- **In Teams Chats:** Share a checklist or notes directly in a Teams chat to collaborate live during meetings.

- **In Outlook Emails:** Embed tables, checklists, or task lists into Outlook emails to ensure everyone works with real-time content.

- **In Word Documents:** Use Loop Components within Word documents for collaborative updates.

Tip: Copy the component link from your Loop Page and paste it directly into Teams or Outlook. Updates will sync automatically across all platforms.

4. Turn Brainstorms into Actionable Tasks

Loop makes it easy to turn messy brainstorming sessions into clear, organized action items.

- Start with a Notes Component to capture ideas as they come.

- Use comments to refine ideas and suggest improvements.

- Convert key ideas into a Checklist Component or a Table to assign tasks and deadlines.

Example: During a brainstorming session, Sarah's team listed ideas in a Notes Component. After the meeting, Sarah turned those ideas into a task list with owners and due dates, keeping the project moving forward.

5. Leverage Copilot for Smarter Collaboration

Copilot, Microsoft's AI assistant, is a game-changer in Loop. Use it to:

- **Summarize Notes:** Copilot can turn long meeting notes into concise summaries with key takeaways.

- **Generate Task Lists:** Ask Copilot to extract action items from brainstorming pages or meeting minutes.

- **Suggest Content:** If you're unsure where to start, Copilot can suggest relevant components, structures, or formats for your Loop Pages.

Tip: Try typing a simple prompt like *"Summarize this page into a checklist of action items"* or *"What are the key points from this meeting?"*

6. Keep Your Workspaces Tidy with Structure

While Loop offers flexibility, maintaining structure is key to keeping your workspaces productive.

- **Use Sections and Headings:** Organize pages with clear headings and sections to break up content.

- **Group Related Pages:** Keep similar pages together within a workspace to make navigation easier.

- **Archive Old Pages:** Move completed projects or outdated pages to an "Archived" folder so they don't clutter your active workspace.

Example: Sarah kept her Loop Workspace tidy by creating folders for brainstorming, task tracking, and meeting notes, making it easy for her team to find what they needed.

7. Track Updates with Comments and Mentions

Stay on top of collaboration by using comments and mentions to bring clarity and accountability to your Loop content.

- **Add Comments:** Highlight specific text or components and add comments for feedback or clarification.

- **Tag Team Members:** Use "@mentions" to notify teammates of updates, questions, or tasks requiring their input.

- **Resolve Comments:** Once a discussion is complete, mark the comment as resolved to keep the page clean.

Tip: Use comments to keep conversations organized instead of editing content directly.

8. Make Use of Templates

Save time and maintain consistency by using Loop templates to get started quickly. While templates may be simple, they're a great way to standardize processes and structures across your team.

- Common Templates:

  - **Meeting Notes**: Pre-structured notes for agenda, decisions, and action items.

  - **Project Tracker**: Ready-made tables to monitor project progress.

  - **Task Lists**: Templates for assigning and tracking tasks.

Example: Sarah's team used a "Weekly Team Sync" template to create standardized meeting agendas, making every check-in efficient and effective.

9. Collaborate Asynchronously

Loop enables seamless asynchronous collaboration—perfect for teams in different time zones or those working on flexible schedules.

- Use Loop Pages as a single source of truth, where updates happen in real time.

- Encourage team members to leave comments, notes, or updates at their convenience.

- Summarize progress with Copilot to keep everyone aligned, even if they're not working at the same time.

Example: Sarah's global team used a Loop Page to track updates on a project. Each team member added updates as they worked, and Copilot summarized the changes for a quick, unified view.

10. Regularly Review and Optimize Your Flows

Just like any productivity tool, it's important to review how your team is using Microsoft Loop and refine your workflows as needed.

- Periodically clean up workspaces to remove unused components or pages.

- Look for ways to improve workflows: Are there repetitive tasks Copilot could automate?

- Encourage feedback: Ask your team what's working well and what could be improved.

These tips and tricks will help you unlock the full power of Microsoft Loop, transforming how you and your team collaborate. By working smarter, organizing effectively, and leveraging AI tools like Copilot, you'll create a seamless and productive environment for your projects.

AI-POWERED COLLABORATION

As collaboration evolves, so does the technology that supports it. Enter Copilot, Microsoft's AI-powered assistant that integrates seamlessly with Microsoft Loop to make teamwork smarter, faster, and more efficient. Copilot simplifies content creation, streamlines workflows, and even helps you stay organized by offering AI-generated suggestions, summaries, and solutions—all in real time.

In this chapter, we'll explore the many ways Copilot enhances Microsoft Loop, from generating content and streamlining tasks to its newest innovation—Copilot Pages, a game-changing feature that allows you to share chats and insights seamlessly in your Loop Workspaces.

Copilot is like having a digital assistant built into Microsoft Loop. It uses the power of AI to help you create, organize, and manage content effortlessly. Whether you're starting a project, refining ideas, or summarizing updates, Copilot is there to assist you every step of the way.

With Copilot, you can:

1. **Summarize Content:** Automatically extract key points from long notes or discussions.

2. **Generate Action Items:** Turn brainstorming sessions into clear, structured to-dos.

3. **Draft Content Quickly:** Ask Copilot to create notes, task lists, or progress trackers based on your input.

4. **Streamline Updates:** Let Copilot highlight changes, provide recommendations, or clean up cluttered content.

Copilot is more than just a helper—it's a proactive collaborator that saves time and ensures your team stays aligned.

Loop Components are where much of the action happens, and Copilot takes their functionality to the next level:

- **Automate Checklists:** Copilot can generate task lists based on meeting notes, helping you turn discussions into actionable items.

- **Summarize Table Data:** If you're working with a Loop table, Copilot can analyze the content and provide quick summaries or key insights.

- **Refine Notes:** Instead of sifting through long-winded notes, ask Copilot to summarize or rewrite content in a clear, concise way.

Example: After a team brainstorming session, Sarah asked Copilot to generate a checklist of action items based on the meeting notes in her Loop Page. Copilot quickly pulled out the relevant to-dos and presented them in a clean, actionable format.

One of the newest and most exciting features of Copilot in Loop is Copilot Pages. This innovative tool bridges the gap between your Copilot chat history and your Loop Workspaces, allowing you to seamlessly bring AI-powered insights into your projects.

Here's how Copilot Pages work:

- When you interact with Copilot in apps like Teams or other Microsoft tools, the AI generates summaries, suggestions, or ideas based on your conversations.

- With the new Pages feature, you can now take these chats, summaries, or insights and share them directly into your Loop Workspace as a Loop Page.

- These Copilot-generated Pages can serve as a starting point for project planning, brainstorming sessions, or task lists.

Why This Matters:

- **Eliminates Duplication:** You no longer need to manually copy and paste insights from Copilot into your workspace. Everything integrates seamlessly.

- **Increases Context Sharing:** Insights from Copilot chats—such as meeting takeaways or project notes—are instantly accessible to your entire team in the Loop Workspace.

- **Saves Time:** Instead of recreating discussions, teams can work from AI-generated summaries and refine them collaboratively.

Example: Sarah had an insightful chat with Copilot in Microsoft Teams about improving her team's content workflow. Copilot provided a summary of her conversation with action points. Sarah then shared this summary into her Loop Workspace as a new Copilot Page, where her team could collaborate further.

Let's look at practical ways you can leverage Copilot's AI magic to enhance your Loop experience:

1. **Brainstorming Sessions:**
   - Start with a blank Loop Page and let Copilot help you brainstorm ideas. Simply type, "Generate five ideas for a marketing strategy," and watch as Copilot delivers a list to spark creativity.

2. **Meeting Summaries:**
   - After a meeting, use Copilot to summarize notes into clear action points. Share these as a Loop Component to ensure your team stays aligned.

3. **Content Drafting:**
   - Need a first draft of a report, checklist, or progress tracker? Ask Copilot to generate content on your behalf and refine it as needed.

4. **Project Updates:**
   - Use Copilot to summarize the progress on a Loop Page, such as "Summarize tasks completed this week" or "Highlight any overdue items in this table."

5. **Knowledge Sharing:**
    o Turn your Copilot chats into actionable Copilot Pages that live in your workspace for your team to use and build upon.

Tips for Making the Most of Copilot in Loop

- **Be Specific with Prompts:** The clearer your question or request, the better Copilot's response will be. For example: "Summarize key tasks from this meeting" works better than "What's next?"

- **Iterate and Refine:** If Copilot doesn't deliver exactly what you need, refine your request. Follow up with prompts like "Make this more concise" or "Add bullet points."

- **Collaborate on Copilot Pages:** Once you add a Copilot Page to your Loop Workspace, let your team refine or build on the content collaboratively.

Addressing Common Questions About Copilot in Loop

Is Copilot reliable for complex projects?
Yes! While Copilot simplifies content creation, it's best to review and refine AI-generated content for complex projects to ensure it meets your team's standards.

Can I customize Copilot suggestions?
Absolutely. Copilot's output is fully editable, allowing you to adjust or personalize suggestions to suit your needs.

Is Copilot secure?
Yes. Copilot operates within Microsoft's robust security framework, ensuring your content and insights are protected.

With Copilot in Microsoft Loop, you no longer have to wrestle with blank pages, endless updates, or scattered ideas. Copilot simplifies the entire process, helping you create, organize, and share content in ways that were never possible before. It brings speed, clarity, and innovation to every step of your workflow, making collaboration easier and more productive.

- **For Individuals:** Copilot acts as your personal assistant, streamlining content creation and organization.

- **For Teams:** Copilot enhances collaboration by summarizing, generating, and integrating insights across apps and workspaces.

By now, you can see how Copilot isn't just a tool—it's a collaborative partner that makes Microsoft Loop even more powerful.

COMMON PITFALLS AND HOW TO AVOID THEM

Microsoft Loop is a powerful tool that can transform the way individuals and teams collaborate. However, like any technology, it's easy to run into challenges if you're not familiar with its nuances or best practices. Whether it's disorganized workspaces, misused Loop Components, or integration confusion, these pitfalls can slow you down and prevent you from getting the most out of Loop.

In this chapter, we'll explore the most common issues users face and provide practical solutions to help you avoid them. By learning how to sidestep these challenges, you can keep your Loop experience smooth, productive, and frustration-free.

1. Creating Too Many Workspaces

The Pitfall:
It's easy to create multiple workspaces for every project, task, or idea, but too many workspaces can quickly become overwhelming. Users may struggle to find relevant information, and important pages could get buried in the clutter.

How to Avoid It:

- **Consolidate Workspaces:** Create one workspace for related projects or teams instead of separate ones for every minor task.

- **Name Workspaces Clearly:** Use descriptive names like *"Q2 Marketing Plan"* or *"Product Launch Project"* to make them easy to identify.

- **Archive Old Workspaces:** Once a project is complete, archive the workspace to declutter your Loop environment.

Example: Sarah initially created separate workspaces for each phase of her marketing project. After her team grew overwhelmed, she consolidated them into one "Marketing Hub" workspace with organized pages for each phase.

2. Overloading Loop Pages

The Pitfall:
While Loop Pages are flexible and dynamic, adding too much content—like multiple components, files, and notes—can make them cluttered and difficult to navigate.

How to Avoid It:

- **One Page, One Purpose:** Each page should have a clear goal (e.g., brainstorming, meeting notes, or task tracking). Avoid turning a single page into a catch-all.

- **Use Headings and Sections:** Break content into clear, logical sections to make pages easy to scan.

- **Split Content Across Pages:** If a page feels too long, split it into smaller pages and link them together.

Example: Sarah's "Project Updates" page became too cluttered with notes, tables, and links. To fix this, she split it into smaller pages—one for meeting notes, another for the task list, and one for key milestones.

3. Misusing Loop Components

The Pitfall:
Loop Components are incredibly versatile, but it's easy to misuse them—such as embedding too many in a single page or sharing components without context. This can create confusion and disjointed workflows.

How to Avoid It:

- **Choose the Right Component:** Use checklists for to-dos, tables for structured data, and notes for brainstorming. Avoid unnecessary complexity.

- **Share with Context:** When embedding a component in Teams or Outlook, explain its purpose and how team members should interact with it.

- **Keep Components Focused:** Don't overload a single component with too much information; keep it concise and actionable.

Example: Sarah embedded a table component in her team's chat without context, and no one knew how to use it. She added a short note explaining, *"Here's our project status tracker. Please update your task progress by EOD."*

4. Failing to Use Notifications and Comments

The Pitfall:
Loop excels at real-time collaboration, but if team members don't communicate effectively—like missing updates or failing to leave comments—important changes may go unnoticed.

How to Avoid It:

- **Use @Mentions:** Tag teammates using "@" to notify them of updates, questions, or areas that need their attention.

- **Comment, Don't Edit Directly:** For feedback or suggestions, use comments instead of overwriting content. This keeps the original content intact while tracking changes.

- **Set Expectations:** Encourage your team to check for notifications and updates regularly.

Example: Sarah added comments to her team's brainstorming notes instead of making edits. This allowed everyone to see her suggestions without losing the original ideas.

5. Ignoring Integration Opportunities

The Pitfall:
Some users treat Microsoft Loop as an isolated tool, missing out on its powerful integration with other Microsoft 365 apps like Teams, Outlook, Word, and OneDrive.

How to Avoid It:

- **Embed Components in Teams:** Use Loop Components in Teams chats or channels for real-time collaboration.

- **Include Loop in Outlook:** Share Loop Components in emails so content stays updated without back-and-forth messaging.

- **Leverage Copilot Pages:** Share Copilot chat summaries into your Loop Workspace to capture key ideas or tasks.

Example: Sarah used Loop Components in both her Teams chat and Outlook emails to share real-time project updates. Her team saved time by staying aligned without switching apps.

6. Neglecting Copilot's Capabilities

The Pitfall:
Some users forget to leverage Copilot's AI features in Microsoft Loop, missing out on its ability to streamline workflows, generate content, and summarize updates.

How to Avoid It:

- **Summarize Notes:** After meetings or brainstorming sessions, use Copilot to summarize key points and create action items.

- **Generate Content:** Ask Copilot to draft ideas, checklists, or structured outlines when you're stuck.

- **Use Copilot Pages:** Share Copilot-generated chat summaries or insights into your Loop Workspace to keep the team aligned.

Example: Sarah used Copilot to turn a long brainstorming session into a clear action plan. She then shared the AI-generated Copilot Page in her Loop Workspace for her team to refine.

7. Lack of Structure in Workflows

The Pitfall:
Without clear structure or workflow processes, Loop can quickly become chaotic, making it harder for teams to collaborate effectively.

How to Avoid It:

- **Set Guidelines:** Define how your team will use Loop (e.g., naming conventions, component placement, update frequency).

- **Assign Ownership:** Designate team members to manage pages or update components.

- **Review Regularly:** Periodically revisit Loop Workspaces to clean up outdated content and optimize structure.

Example: Sarah's team agreed to a workflow where Loop task lists would be updated every Friday. This kept their project tracker current without micromanagement.

8. Overlooking Privacy and Permissions

The Pitfall:
While Loop makes collaboration seamless, it's important to be mindful of sharing sensitive or private information. Misconfigured permissions can lead to unauthorized access or content edits.

How to Avoid It:

- **Check Permissions:** Before sharing a workspace or component, ensure permissions are set appropriately (e.g., view-only or edit access).

- **Secure Sensitive Content:** Avoid sharing confidential data in shared components unless necessary.

- **Monitor Activity:** Regularly review activity in shared Loop Workspaces to ensure everything is secure.

Example: Sarah created a private workspace for her team's financial planning and restricted permissions to trusted team members.

Every tool has its challenges, but by understanding these common pitfalls and learning how to avoid them, you can unlock the full potential of Microsoft Loop. Whether it's keeping workspaces organized, using Loop Components effectively, or leveraging Copilot for smarter workflows, these best practices will ensure a smooth, productive experience.

BRINGING MICROSOFT LOOP TO LIFE

Sarah sat at her desk, staring at the growing list of emails, Teams messages, and scattered documents that cluttered her day. It was Monday morning, and her team's big presentation was due on Friday. The stakes were high: a new client had tasked them with creating a detailed strategy for launching their product line, and Sarah, as the team lead, felt the weight of responsibility pressing down on her.

The problem wasn't her team's skills or effort—they were a talented group. The issue was communication. Task lists were buried in emails, meeting notes were lost in different documents, and everyone seemed to be working on their own isolated version of the plan.

"We're wasting so much time chasing information instead of actually working," she muttered to herself. Something had to change.

That morning, during the team's virtual meeting, Sarah introduced Microsoft Loop to her team. She had spent the weekend exploring it and was excited to see how it could solve their problems.

"Guys, we need a central place to collaborate—one that updates in real time," she said, sharing her screen. "I've set up a Loop Workspace for this project. Everything we need—task lists, notes, ideas—will live here, and it will stay updated no matter where we're working. It's like one tool to connect all our tools."

Her team was skeptical. Another tool? They already used so many. But as Sarah walked them through it, a spark of interest ignited.

Sarah created a Loop Page titled *"Project Launch Strategy,"* where she:

1. Inserted a Task List Component for action items.

2. Added a Notes Component for brainstorming ideas.

3. Embedded a Table Component to track deadlines, responsibilities, and milestones.

"This isn't just another static document," she explained. "You can update these components directly from Teams or Outlook, and the changes will sync everywhere."

"Wait," Mark, the creative lead, interrupted. "So if I update the task list in Teams, it shows up here too?"

"Exactly," Sarah smiled. "No more back-and-forth emails or 'final-final' documents."

As the week progressed, the team began to see the magic of Loop.

- **Monday Afternoon:**
  Mark started brainstorming campaign ideas directly in the *"Brainstorming Notes"* section of the workspace. Sarah chimed in with comments, while the project manager, Priya, turned key ideas into actionable tasks within the same page.

"This feels like we're in the same room working together," Priya said, amazed.

- **Tuesday Morning:**
  Sarah shared a Loop Table Component in their Microsoft Teams chat to track progress. Mark updated his status to *"In Progress,"* while Priya flagged two tasks that needed immediate attention. Sarah received real-time updates without having to ask anyone for status reports.

"This is saving me so much time," she said to herself.

- **Wednesday Evening:**
  During their midweek check-in, Sarah leveraged Copilot in Microsoft Loop to summarize brainstorming notes from the past few days. Copilot neatly organized the team's discussions into a list of clear action items and tasks.

"Copilot just turned a wall of text into a workable plan," Mark said, impressed.

Sarah took things a step further and used Copilot Pages to share insights from a Teams chat she'd had with the client earlier that day. Instead of manually summarizing the conversation, Copilot generated a Loop Page with key takeaways, which she seamlessly added to the workspace for the team to review.

"Now everyone's in the loop—no pun intended," she joked.

By Thursday, everything seemed on track. The tasks were progressing, deadlines were being met, and the team felt more organized than ever. Then, Priya noticed a problem. The client had updated the requirements, and two key deliverables needed a major adjustment.

Sarah panicked for a moment, but then she remembered the flexibility of Loop.

"Let's jump into the workspace," she told the team in their emergency Teams call. "We'll adjust the plan together."

Within minutes:

- Priya updated the table to reflect the new requirements.
- Mark adjusted the creative brainstorming notes to align with the changes.
- Sarah updated the task list to reprioritize the work.

Thanks to Loop's real-time sync, everyone saw the updates immediately. There was no confusion, no duplicate documents, and no wasted time.

"We're going to pull this off," Sarah said with confidence.

On Friday morning, the team walked into the client's virtual meeting with confidence. Their plan was polished, cohesive, and clear. Sarah presented directly from their Loop Workspace, pulling up the updated notes, status table, and deliverables that reflected their week of hard work.

The client was thrilled. "This is exactly what we were hoping for— detailed, flexible, and organized," they said.

After the meeting, Sarah sat back and smiled. It had been a challenging week, but Microsoft Loop had transformed the way her team worked.

- Communication was clear and connected.

- Information was always up to date, no matter where it lived.

- Copilot had saved time by summarizing notes and generating insights.

- Collaboration had never felt so seamless.

"This isn't just a tool," Sarah thought. "It's how teamwork should feel—connected, dynamic, and effortless."

Sarah's story is one many teams can relate to—struggling with scattered information, missed updates, and the stress of tight deadlines. But by adopting Microsoft Loop, her team unlocked a new way to collaborate, one that emphasized:

1. **Real-Time Synchronization:** Every update, no matter where it was made, synced instantly across all platforms.

2. **Dynamic Content:** Loop Components turned static notes and lists into living, breathing content that evolved with their needs.

3. **AI Assistance with Copilot:** Copilot helped summarize, organize, and simplify complex workflows, saving hours of manual effort.

4. **Team Unity:** Loop Workspaces brought everyone together in one place, turning chaos into clarity.

Sarah's journey with Microsoft Loop is more than just a success story—it's an example of what's possible when teams embrace tools designed for the modern workplace. Whether you're leading a project, managing a team, or organizing your personal workflow, Loop can help you stay connected, aligned, and productive.

YOUR JOURNEY WITH MICROSOFT LOOP

Microsoft Loop isn't just another collaboration tool; it's a bridge connecting teams, ideas, and content in ways that feel intuitive, organized, and seamless. Throughout this book, we've explored Loop's dynamic features, real-world use cases, and its ability to bring clarity and efficiency to the modern workplace. Whether you're managing a team project, organizing personal workflows, or integrating with tools like Copilot, Microsoft Loop transforms the way you work.

Let's take a moment to reflect on what we've covered and how Sarah's journey mirrors the transformative power of Loop—one that you, as a learner and user, can experience too.

What We've Learned

1. **Introduction to Microsoft Loop**
   We started by understanding the importance of Loop in today's collaborative environment. As work becomes increasingly remote, complex, and fast-paced, the need for a unified, flexible workspace is more pressing than ever. Loop addresses these challenges by enabling real-time collaboration, integration, and organization across Microsoft 365.

2. **What is Microsoft Loop?**
   We broke down Loop into its core components:

   o **Loop Components:** Modular, real-time elements like checklists, tables, and notes that update everywhere they live.

   o **Loop Pages:** Flexible canvases to organize content and ideas collaboratively.

- o **Loop Workspaces:** Shared spaces that bring related pages and components together for team projects.

We saw how Loop Components can live across Microsoft Teams, Outlook, and other apps, ensuring that updates are dynamic and always in sync.

3. **Why Use Microsoft Loop?**
   From reducing version chaos to enabling real-time updates, Loop stands out by making collaboration efficient, reducing redundancy, and empowering teams to stay aligned—no matter where they work. Integration across the Microsoft 365 ecosystem amplifies its value.

4. **Getting Started with Loop**
   Practical steps were shared to help you set up your first workspace, create pages, and embed Loop Components. You learned that Loop is both simple to use and endlessly adaptable for any project or workflow.

5. **Best Practices and Tips**
   We explored strategies for keeping workspaces tidy, using Loop Components effectively, and leveraging features like comments and mentions to stay organized. Tips for using templates, working asynchronously, and integrating Copilot ensured you're set up for success.

6. **Copilot in Microsoft Loop**
   One of Loop's most exciting features is its integration with Copilot. Whether summarizing meeting notes, generating task lists, or leveraging the new Copilot Pages feature to bring chats into Loop Workspaces, Copilot helps streamline workflows and saves valuable time.

7. **Common Pitfalls and How to Avoid Them**
   We tackled the challenges users often face—like cluttered workspaces, misused components, and lack of structure—and provided actionable solutions to overcome these obstacles.

8. **The Episode: Sarah's Journey**
   Sarah's story illustrated how Loop can transform a team's workflow, taking them from scattered information and miscommunication to clear, collaborative, and productive teamwork.

Sarah's experience with Microsoft Loop reflects the journey that many of us take when exploring new tools. Like Sarah, you may feel overwhelmed at first—juggling emails, outdated files, and disconnected conversations. But Sarah's story shows how Loop can bring order to chaos, streamline collaboration, and create a single source of truth for any project.

In her story:

- Loop Components became her team's lifeline, syncing real-time updates across Teams and Outlook.
- Loop Workspaces provided a unified hub where her team could brainstorm, track tasks, and share progress.
- Copilot helped summarize insights, organize content, and create actionable steps, saving the team precious time.

Sarah's journey mirrors your own path as you explore Loop. It's normal to face a learning curve when adopting a new tool, but the rewards are worth it. With Loop, you can:

- Break free from scattered workflows and embrace organization.
- Turn static content into living, evolving ideas.
- Empower yourself and your team to collaborate better, smarter, and faster.

Just like Sarah's team delivered a winning presentation, you too can achieve results that feel effortless yet impactful.

As you finish this book, think about your own projects, workflows, or teams. Where could Microsoft Loop make a difference?

- Are you juggling too many versions of a task list? Try a Loop Component.

- Do your meeting notes disappear into a sea of emails? Use a shared Loop Page.

- Are you looking for smarter ways to summarize and organize content? Lean on Copilot to simplify the work.

Loop isn't just about transforming your projects—it's about transforming the way you approach collaboration. With its real-time sync, AI-powered tools, and flexibility, Microsoft Loop becomes more than just another app. It's a workspace where your ideas, tasks, and people connect seamlessly.

As we wrap up this chapter, remember that Microsoft Loop is just one part of the Microsoft 365 ecosystem. Tools like Teams, Outlook, OneDrive, and more work alongside Loop to create a complete, connected environment for modern work.

This book is part of the Microsoft 365 Companion Series, designed to help you unlock the power of each app. Whether it's SharePoint, OneNote, Teams, or Word, these resources are here to guide you step-by-step on your learning journey.

The key to success? Never stop learning. Technology evolves, and tools like Loop are designed to evolve with you. By staying curious, experimenting with features, and embracing new possibilities, you'll continue to grow and thrive in today's fast-paced, ever-changing world of work.

So, what are you waiting for? Dive in, explore, and let Microsoft Loop transform the way you work—just like it did for Sarah and her team.

Your journey is only just beginning. Let's get to work!

THE POWER OF TRANSFORMATION WITH MICROSOFT LOOP

As we come to the close of this book, one thing is clear: Microsoft Loop is more than just a collaboration tool—it's a gateway to a smarter, more connected way of working. It transforms how you organize ideas, track progress, and collaborate with your team, offering a level of flexibility and dynamism that modern workflows demand.

But this isn't just about technology. It's about what you can achieve when armed with the right tools. Microsoft Loop helps you and your team stay aligned, productive, and innovative, no matter how complex the project or how far apart you may be.

Throughout this book, we've explored Loop from every angle:

- Understanding what it is and how its components, pages, and workspaces bring ideas to life.

- Learning why it matters, with real-world scenarios showing how Loop simplifies workflows, eliminates redundant tasks, and enables seamless collaboration.

- Taking those first steps to set up your workspaces, create pages, and embed components that sync across Microsoft Teams, Outlook, and more.

- Embracing best practices and tips and tricks to make the most of Loop's dynamic features, while avoiding the common pitfalls that can slow you down.

- Seeing how tools like Copilot add AI-powered intelligence to Loop, saving time and helping you focus on what matters most.

- Experiencing Sarah's story—a real-life illustration of Loop's transformative power—and reflecting on how her journey mirrors your own learning experience.

Loop isn't just about getting things done. It's about doing them better, smarter, and faster, all while staying organized and focused.

While Loop is revolutionary, it's just one piece of a much larger puzzle. Microsoft 365 is a rich ecosystem of tools that work together seamlessly to meet the needs of today's modern workplace:

- Teams connects your conversations and meetings.

- Outlook keeps you organized and informed.

- OneDrive stores your files securely in the cloud.

- SharePoint acts as a central hub for content and collaboration.

- OneNote, Word, PowerPoint, and Excel give you tools to write, present, and analyze like a pro.

Microsoft Loop ties all of these tools together. Its real-time synchronization, embedded components, and flexibility allow you to stay connected no matter where or how you work. By learning Loop, you're not just mastering a new tool—you're learning how to make the entire Microsoft 365 suite work smarter for you.

Technology doesn't stand still, and neither should you. Microsoft Loop—and tools like it—are always evolving, and the true power lies in staying curious, adaptable, and committed to learning.

This book has given you the foundation to get started with Microsoft Loop, but your journey doesn't end here. As you continue to explore and use Loop:

- Experiment with its features. Push the limits of what it can do.

- Embrace AI tools like Copilot to supercharge your workflows.

- Share your knowledge with your team and encourage them to grow alongside you.

Remember Sarah's story: her team didn't just survive a chaotic project— they thrived because they adopted a tool that empowered them to work better together. That same transformation is within your reach, too.

Microsoft Loop is just the beginning. Each app in the Microsoft 365 suite offers its own unique capabilities, waiting to be unlocked. From managing projects in Planner to creating stunning presentations in PowerPoint or collaborating in SharePoint, the tools are there to help you achieve your goals.

The Microsoft 365 Companion Series is designed to support you on that journey. Each book takes you step-by-step through a different app, making complex tools easy to understand and helping you use them to their full potential.

Whether you're exploring Microsoft Teams, mastering OneNote, or learning how Copilot enhances your productivity, there's always more to learn.

Microsoft Loop is about more than just collaboration—it's about transformation. It's about transforming the way you work, the way your team connects, and the way ideas evolve into results.

So, take what you've learned and put it into action. Start with a simple workspace, create a page, or embed your first Loop Component in Teams. You don't need to have all the answers right away—just start, experiment, and grow.

This is your moment to redefine how you work, communicate, and collaborate. Let Microsoft Loop guide you toward a future where productivity feels seamless, teamwork feels effortless, and your ideas come to life.

The tools are ready. The journey is yours. Let's get started.

www.ingramcontent.com/pod-product-compliance
Lightning Source LLC
LaVergne TN
LVHW051617050326
832903LV00033B/4538